L i f t   Y o u r
Spirits

My Journey Through
Panic Attacks

Noni Gove

After eight years of searching for an answer to release nocturnal panic attacks, the author finally found the solution. Here is her story of never giving up hope, keeping an open mind and pressing on with life to the full, regardless of debilitating circumstances.

BALBOA.
PRESS
A DIVISION OF HAY HOUSE

Balboa Press books may be ordered through booksellers or by contacting:

Balboa Press
A Division of Hay House
1663 Liberty Drive
Bloomington, IN 47403
www.balboapress.com.au
1-(877) 407-4847

ISBN: 978-1-4525-0392-9 (sc)
ISBN: 978-1-4525-0393-6 (e)

Printed in the United States of America

Balboa Press rev. date: 02/08/2012

To my very good friend,
Gerda Foster

1995

A very vivid memory from the early hours, 2am to be exact, of Wednesday 15th October 1995, brings me to write about this particular journey in my life. I faced my demons, not knowing what the hell was happening to me and not at that stage thinking for a minute that it would last for two hours and to a lesser degree on and off over the next eight years.

Living on my own had not been a problem for me after my divorce five years earlier. This night I woke in terror, I thought to phone an ambulance but I also thought, I will be dead by the time they got here. I really thought I was dying, what ran through my mind was "well I have no debts, I don't owe anyone anything, my kids are up and running and leading their own lives, so it is OK for me to go". Was this what a heart attack felt like, was this shaking throughout my body going to end in a stroke or paralysis of some kind, was my head about to explode and my brain to shatter into a thousand pieces, like a light globe going off in sparks? Was this shortness of breath going to tighten my throat and cut off the airways altogether? Was I going to end up as a puddle of water from the sweat that was pouring from my body? Would any one find me or would I just evaporate in to thin air, or a heap of ash, like those mysterious self combustions?

The sheer horror of the situation stunned me into a state of a blubbering mess. I wasn't thinking straight, I almost wanted to die, yet feared it, wanted to seek help but didn't know how, wanted to move but my body felt as if it was no longer a part of me.

These thoughts and feelings are as strong today as they were sixteen years ago. After those two hours in October 1995 my mind and body said enough, enough. I finally must have drifted off to sleep thinking, if I wake up I wake up, if I don't I don't. I was happy either way.

When I finally woke up, I had the feeling I had been run over by a heavy truck or was it a steam roller? I had no energy and realised there was no way I could face up to doing the six hours of remedial massage that my clients had booked in for that day. There was no way I could help myself, let alone anyone else. I was flat out putting one foot after the other, I felt I had been through a wringer or was it a mangle, and several times at that. I rang and cancelled all my clients for that day. It was the only time I did that. When I commit to something, I like to give it one hundred percent and I really don't like letting people down. I feel I have failed them in some way.

For a few years I felt embarrassed to tell anyone about my experience. I thought they would think I had gone off my head, or worse still was making it up. I feared no one would believe me, so I just got on with my life as best I could. Plus the fact I was not sure what had happened to me though it was frighteningly real at the time. My energy my body, breathlessness and heart palpitations, neck and shoulder sweats and pain in my sternum again in the early hours of Wednesday morning. A feeling of weakness and lethargy always accompanied these attacks the next day. I went to a homeopath, he gave me some Rescue Remedy, which was to become my main stay for years after with other homeopathic remedies. They did help a little but these nights did persist.

At home I went to see my GP, who told me I was suffering from rigors. I asked him if that was anything to do with rigor mortis, he assured me it wasn't. I had chest x-rays, blood tests, urine and stool tests and checks for tropical diseases. He put me on medication to calm me down, sometimes it worked but mostly it didn't. I also went to Sydney to have Live Blood Analysis, which showed my immune system was low but not much else to worry about . . . well there was Candida Albicans, heart stress, general toxicity, heavy metal toxicity and allergies were picked up. My GP sent me to a cardiologist for an echocardiograph and ECG, to find out that I had hypertrophy of the left ventricle of the heart but it did not warrant treatment.

I continued to be pursued by symptoms but, luckily, not with as much violence as the first attack but enough to make me very aware that something was way out of balance in my mind and body and I had to seek answers. I continued to search while doing my best to act as if all was well in my world. I accepted that this is how it was right now. I believe that, had I not learned to meditate I would not have managed so well to continue my work, my travels and my life in general. Meditation continues to be a daily ritual for me and has helped in so many ways throughout my life, to cope in all circumstances.

A Listen, Bio Energetic practitioner came to my home to treat patients. The Listen system was computerised and picked up what was out of balance. I found out I was allergic to Wintergreen, I had added it to my massage oil, so I immediately took it out. I had a masseuse working for me each Tuesday and she gave me a massage. I wondered if, when I got a full body massage, whether my system went into overload, contributing to my problems in the early hours of Wednesday. My symptoms improved again for a while but continued to have mild vibrations through my body and a loose bowel movement always seemed to be part of the attack. I also was treated for parasites in my body.

I heard about a very good Naturopath at Berry on the south coast, about one and a half hours away, the first thing she said to me was 'don't put anything in your mouth that comes out of a cow'! In other words I was lactose intolerant. She also told me to go off wheat and sugar and I started taking vitamins, minerals and herbs. About this time numbness was starting in my left jaw, left arm and left thigh, pain in my left ribcage, stiffness in the left side of my neck with a burning sensation going down into my shoulder. My Naturopath suggested I have lymphatic drainage massage, which I would include in my trips to Berry.

At this time a wonderful book came my way, it is called A Path with Heart by Jack Kornfield. Essentially, it became my 'bible', it lived beside my bed and I absorbed every paragraph, over and over. It is still one of my all time favourites. Jack Kornfield is an American, who was a Buddhist monk in Thailand for many years, before disrobing and opening the Spirit Rock Centre in California. I subsequently visited his centre for a Monday night meditation session. About 300 people attend every week, it was simply marvellous.

In 1985, ten years before the nocturnal panic attacks began, I had a really bad fall, when the horse I was riding shied and slipped over on a bitumen road. I got slammed onto the road surface on my left side, with the horse on top of me. He was an ex-racehorse and no light weight, let me tell you. I was leading a group of twenty seven riders, so the only thing to do was pick ourselves up (the horse and I) and get back on with the job. Nothing appeared broken, just badly jolted and shaken. I wondered whether all these left sided symptoms where anything to do with that encounter of coming to a sudden halt on a very hard surface.

In 1991 I was travelling on my own in the Peloponnese, in the southern part of Greece. I had arrived in Monamvasia, a most beautiful medieval city, built in the 12th century. It is really a small island attached to the mainland by a bridge. I booked into Fanny's Guest House for a few nights. It was clean and tidy, quiet and peaceful. In the middle of the first night, I became aware of severe, heavy chest pains and remember being in a sort of half state of being neither awake nor asleep. I felt breathless and shaky but could not bring myself to wake up. It was a scary situation. After what seemed like an eternity I became conscious of my surroundings and whereabouts. It took me a long time to get back to sleep and when I awoke in the morning, I was wrung out and exhausted. I continued my journey.

1996

In January and February 1996 the symptoms were less frequent and not so severe. I thought here at last I am returning to 'normal' health and life. In May I had frequent pain in the left side of my left breast, going into my ribcage. An Ultra Sound proved negative.

In June I lived in Montreal in Canada for three months with my son and daughter. Neither of them wanted to see Gregory Peck, who was speaking at a venue in the city. I decided to jump on the Metro and go by myself. I was seated in the middle of a row, right up close to the stage. It was so exhilarating to be in his presence but towards the end of the show I started having a panic attack. This was unusual as it was early evening and I had not been asleep. I realised it would be awkward getting out passed all the people in my row. I took some rescue remedy and hoped for the best. I came out in a cold sweat with my heart pumping and really missed the talk from then on. Somehow I got myself back to the apartment we were staying in. After that I had a few disturbed nights, feeling of running a temperature, sweats, vibrations and numbness in my left quadriceps, so decided to see a Homeopathic Doctor. He took a very thorough questionnaire of my medical history and experience, prescribed homeopathics and a visit to an Osteopath. I also saw a Chiropractor in California on the way home for back pain. The symptoms were milder for a while. On one of our road trips, we went to Quebec City, which is quite a few hundred miles from Montreal. We had a lovely day of sightseeing, but on the way home both my adult kids felt sleepy and asked me to drive. This should definitely have brought on a panic attack. There was I in my son's left hand drive car, driving on the 'wrong' side of the road, with all the signs in French. Now French was not one of my better subjects at school and that was forty years ago. I took over the wheel my kids went straight to sleep but I managed to get my precious cargo home without a sign of panic.

Back in Australia I had a Hair Analysis with a high reading of copper and low potassium. Years later I am still detoxing from high lead and cadmium. My digestive system has been severely compromised from the overload of heavy metals and despite the fact of being a big water drinker, I was 'massively' dehydrated.

I heard of a doctor in Palm Beach who used a Vega machine to test the body and treat it with homeopathic remedies. He found I had high copper, lead, mercury, aluminium and arsenic, even traces of TB, malaria and glandular fever. It was a long haul from Moss Vale to Palm Beach, especially as I had a very unreliable bright yellow VW Beetle Convertible. Smart though it was with its roof off, it had seen better days and it was always an adventure to see if you arrived at your destination without the NRMA being called in or at worst, towing you to a garage. After several round trips of six to seven hours, I decided to find something closer to home, I also found his treatment too radical and sometimes the symptoms much worse. I just could not tolerant any more pain and anxiety.

A homeopathic doctor moved to Bowral, only fifteen minutes away, he practised on mount Gibraltar. The VW did not like that much better than going to Palm Beach but I only had to get rescued once by the tow truck from there. You see, it did not like hills, especially steep ones. Once again he tried many remedies and like all the others, they worked for a while but then faded out.

In 1993 I was on a Buddhist pilgrimage which started in Nepal, the birth place of the Buddha. He was born in Lombini over 2500 years ago. Nearby at Kapilavasti, I visited the Buddha's father's kingdom. From there I went on to Sarisvati in India, where the Buddha remained for twenty five years. He gave his first discourse in the park at Sanath, just out of Varanasi, where I was staying in a Thai Temple, before heading to Bodh Gaya where he was enlightened.

I was alone in a large room with three or four double bunks in a Thai Monastery in Sanath. The room was secure and locked, it opened onto a quadrangle within the temple. It was my first night, I was tired and weary from a long bus ride the night before with little sleep. I was on the point of falling asleep when I felt these hands on the back of my neck

---

and shoulders. I froze, I wanted to scream but my throat was constricted and no sound would come forth. Was I about to be strangled? Was there a crazy rapist in the room with me?

My body was paralysed with fear, I was totally unable to move or protect myself. I thought I was going to be murdered for sure. My breathing became so rapid that my lungs were at bursting point. My heart was beating like a frenzied African drummer was practising on my chest.

After what seemed like an eternity, I became calm and realised I could 'see' the hands, even though they were behind my back. They were definitely male, with long fingers and knobbly joints, a brownish colour, more like milk coffee, Indian I thought. How is it possible for me to describe them, when they were out of sight? I slowly came to believe they were healing hands and non-threatening. Then I thought how did this man get into my room? I had been awake and would have heard anyone coming in, this phenomena was not possible.

Finally the hands and pressure on my neck and shoulders faded away. I could now venture to move and check out the room in the half light. I slowly, slowly turned over with trepidation, to see if there was a man standing over me. Of course no one was there. I had come out in a cold sweat, the experience was so profound, so real. It makes me shudder, even now after all these years. I am not easily spooked and have a reputation of being an intrepid traveller but this experience scared the living daylights out of me.

Was this a spiritual entity that visited me, was he male, could it have been the Buddha himself, was he giving me a blessing or healing? Why would he choose this stranger in a foreign land? How did I attract this experience and why? So many unanswered questions.

Many years ago I had read about spiritual entities but had never had a personal experience before this. There were many more to come.

1997

By 1997 the pain and numbness in my left side, especially in bed at night were getting worse, as were the leg cramps. As a consequence my sleep pattern was disturbed and the pain in my sternum was going through to my spine. If I ran for a bus, getting mildly breathless, then sat down, I would get a severe spinal spasm. The only way I could get relief was to stand up and stretch my arms above my head and stretch backwards. Getting breathless on the tennis court had no impact, it was only if I sat down. My tongue and head were slightly enlarged, as was my ribcage. I had numerous sore throats and swollen salivary glands plus tinnitus in my left ear. The nocturnal loose bowel movements persisted. It was so frustrating not to know what was really going on. My awareness was heightened and I felt I was very tuned into my body . . . how could I escape it.

A specialist Holistic Dentist in Sydney diagnosed mercury poisoning from the fourteen or so amalgam fillings I had in my teeth and suggested I have all my amalgam fillings removed. It is a very expensive and prolonged operation over four weeks. I opted for postponing the procedure, taking vitamins, minerals and selenium for six months. Five years later I did have all the amalgam removed and replaced by a compatible filling material. More on that later.

I continued to take homeopathics and for a couple of months there was a general improvement but new symptoms surfaced, like tingling in my hands, fluttering in my muscles, which can crop up any where throughout the body, lower abdominal pain, a feeling of heat in my face, as if I was running a temperature, when in actual fact I had, and still have, a low temperature and heaviness in my left side. The usual panic attacks caused my left eye to be difficult to open in the morning, on waking and the night vibrations through the body with loose bowel movements, in the middle of the night, diminished but by no means left me completely.

For the lower back pain, I went to a local Chiropractor, he also helped with the disturbed sleep and the feeling of weakness that I felt after a bad night. Towards the end of the year I got a bladder infection and had to go onto antibiotics. In India I also visited a Tibetan Herbal Doctor and there was a slight improvement while I was travelling. When I got home, it was back to more of the same. I developed a red 'spidery' rash with white pimples on my right breast. It was heading towards my nipple. After a biopsy from a skin specialist, the prognosis came back . . . hookworm. I wanted to go to a vet and have a dose of Thibenzol. I knew about hookworms in sheep and it worked for them. The skin specialist wasn't so sure. She sold me some very expensive cream and, guess what? . . . . it was called Thibendazol. It worked.

My GP ordered more blood, urine and stool tests. They came back normal. An abdominal ultra sound showed an abnormality in the left kidney but nothing serious. A Pap smear showed an abnormality, so off I went to a gynaecologist, who did a colposcopy and curette. Still the panic attacks persisted. My next referral was to a top neurologist in Sydney. That was not a pleasant experience, to put it mildly. His receptionist was sharp and practical, getting me to pay before I saw the doctor. I was told to wait in his room and there I sat for over half an hour, staring into space, with not even an out dated Readers Digest to read. I meditated, then a gentleman entered the room, finally, did not look at me, make eye contact or tell me his name or ask me mine or acknowledge me in any way, I presumed he was the neurologist. After a few questions and telling me to walk on a line on the floor, he told me to 'go home, calm down and have some stress management'! An expensive exercise with no results and in fact rubbing salt into the wounds.

Towards the end of the year I visited Thailand again, not only to enjoy my 'special island' but to teach English in a Buddhist Monastery for high school age novice monks. I shared my sleeping quarters with a female Thai teacher. She was in the next room of a small two bedroom cottage. I was sleeping on my side on a mat on the floor when I felt these two strong thumbs digging into my back. This spirit's body was pressing against me with a pillow in between us. My first thought was that he would take the pillow and suffocate me. The two points where his thumbs dug into my flesh, through to my ribs were agony. Once again my physical body was unable to react, my arms were as heavy as lead and there was no way I could roll over. I was numb with fear, my vocal chords had gone into spasm, and no sound would come out of my mouth. Time passed slowly, my mind eventually calmed down. I was able to 'talk' to the spirit without words. I gently said "What do you want from me?" No answer came. I said 'Please leave me in peace, I have nothing for you here'. I was left in peace but am still left wondering and seeking answers.

The reader may think that these experiences were just bad dreams. I have had many bad dreams over the years but that is all they are. This is a totally different experience and one you can only know by having the experience yourself.

1998

Going into January 1998 I experienced a really severe attack with my teeth chattering and I could hardly breathe. I rang my GP, he said get to the hospital as soon as possible. I was in such a state, I thought it best not to drive, I rang a dear friend and she got out of her bed to drive me to Bowral Hospital where I was admitted, still shaking and shivering. They ran some tests, gave me a sedative and three hours later sent me home. There was another occasion when I drove myself to the same hospital in the early hours of the morning and sat in my car feeling too weak to walk inside. I waited a couple of hours and drove home. All these years I managed to keep my massage clinic open with help from a young friend, who did an excellent job, I continued to play competition tennis, do yoga, walk my dog, mow the lawns, wash the towels, have friends and family to stay and travel overseas. After a particularly bad night I would try to have an afternoon sleep, it was the only way I could get through the day.

Three years down the track from the first encounter, I decided to see an alternate doctor in Bundanoon. He gave me Vitamin B12 injections, they certainly lifted my energy. He also gave me Xanax and Valium to calm me down when I felt an attack coming on. He told me he thought I was having nocturnal panic attacks. At last I had a name for my attacks. Usually I went to sleep at night feeling OK, only to be woken from sleep abruptly by my body vibrating, the usual neck and shoulder sweat, heart palpitations and my left eye closed and hard to open. Mostly an urgent bowel movement accompanied these symptoms. At times these attacks would happen nightly, then weekly or if I was really fortunate, down to fortnightly.

On one of my trips to Thailand I went to the Tropical Diseases Hospital in Bangkok, thinking this may shed some light on something the doctors might have missed or not known about in Australia. The blood test came up normal with the stool tests showing more parasites, which were treated. In Rayong, a large southern city, I was riding a push bike and was bitten by a dog and had to have a tetanus injection. I refused the rabies injection, as I knew the dog and knew it did not have rabies. In Thailand I stayed on my favourite island and had a daily Thai Massage, I meditated, did Qi Gong, a form of Tai Chi, and dipped into the water throughout the day, sometimes snorkelling, which is another world.

Back home a local neurologist suggested a CT brain scan, carotid duplex and thyroid test. They thought I may be suffering mini strokes. The tests came back clear, which was heartening but still did not spell out what was causing the panic attacks. In the Bowral Hospital I had a curette and biopsy followed by antibiotics and much vaginal bleeding. I then took probiotics after I had finished the course of antibiotics. A cardiac stress test was fine and my blood pressure normal. A further test for helicobacter pylori was clear.

One of the most helpful treatments to give me energy was the continued Vitamin B12 injections. I also took liquid iron, potassium, magnesium, calcium, wild yam, choline, vitamin C and E, vitamin B5 and B6, slippery elm, kava, garlic, arsenicum, astragalus and for parasites Hulda Clark's herbal remedies of black walnut hull, wormwood, oil of cloves. I drank two litres of purified water every day. I also got a cousin to make me Hulda Clark's famous 'zapper', which I used for some time. It was to zap the parasites. I also continued to have regular remedial massage from several of my very good friends and chiropractic from a practitioner on the south coast.

In July I travelled with a dear friend to Alaska and Canada, to my son's wedding. The symptoms were milder and I was really able to enjoy my trip, with the help of Rescue Remedy and half a Valium now and then. I started doing Feldenkraus movements when I got home. I was willing to try whatever anyone suggested.

1999

In February 1999 I arrived in my new unit at Bondi Beach. It was a huge 'sea change' and one that I hoped may see a clearing away of the panic attacks and all that went with them.

Nothing changed with my body aches and pains, vibrations, shortness of breath, heat in my face, nocturnal panic attacks, disturbed nights and weakness during the day.

I was running a consistently low body temperature of 35.8 in the morning rising to 36.2 at night. I became conscious of feeling the cold and that is one of the reasons I moved from the Southern Highlands of New South Wales to the coast of Sydney. I noticed that my concentration levels were low but I continued to meditate and do Qi Gong on a regular basis. As the surf was so close, I got plenty of surf, sun, sand and swimming. The palpitations remained and I could feel the pulse through my whole body at times. The heat in my face lasted from hours to days, I had itchy eyes and ears, my dreams were more like nightmares, weird and scary. The left side of my body still had times of numbness, heaviness and muscle fluttering, my thoracic spine was painful. My nights were disturbed by panic attack symptoms, including loose bowel movements, my memory was not trustworthy anymore and when writing I would find I left out words or letters. I sometimes found it hard to swallow and had gut pains, ileo cecal valve spasms and a feeling of bloating in my abdomen. My energy levels were low following disturbed nights and the nocturnal neck sweats at times saw me changing my night wear and pillow slip. My eye sight was sometimes blurry and then there were the sparkling lights to deal with. I am sure that some of the practitioners I went to see thought for sure I was imagining all this, which is one of the reasons I documented it all so clearly.

I continued to meditate, take selenium, barley green, vitamin C and E, Potassium, magnesium, zinc and ate psyllium husks, vegetables, walnuts, sunflower and pumpkin seeds and very little meat. After one or two disturbed nights, I resorted to take a sleeping pill, half a Normison. I have never been one for taking pills but at times they are necessary. I even found Noni Juice, which is meant to cure just about anything. I was sure it would resonate with me. My main exercise was swimming, either at the beach or in the indoor heated pool in my block of units or bogey boarding in the surf. I also had a mountain bike, which I rode round the streets of Bondi until one day a driver in a parked car suddenly opened his car door and I went full tilt in to it and whack onto the road. Shook myself off and got to my favourite coffee shop, where I discovered a cut hand. It could have been much worse. Not long after that I sold the bike.

In March I was in Canada to see my first little granddaughter who was born in December the year before. It was a real challenge to be in temperatures of—24 degrees with a wind chill factor of—36 degrees but it was worth it just to be there with my family and cuddle the little one. I enjoyed Epsom Salt baths and driving a snow mobile for 50 kms, which was exhilarating. It was great to be able to massage most members of the family.

When I got home in April I got a part time job massaging at the Icebergs, just over the road from where I lived. I continue to love my work. I also went to Kensington to massage some retired nuns and St Leonards to attend Psychotherapist lectures. I did seated massage for a Travel Agency staff in the city. A few visits to a Chinese Doctor in Bondi Junction who practised Aura Soma, Kinesiology, herbs and homeopathy was an interesting experience. I attended dream workshops and Kings Cross for the Korean Baths and massage, which I love. While the panic attacks were not so numerous at this time, my body still did not feel right. I often wrote in my diary that I was feeling strange and even losing the plot. It was hard to describe. There were times when I felt nervy and shaky, this was a very strange feeling for me, I had never been a nervous person. I resorted to half a Xanax and or Valium sometimes at night to get a decent sleep.

Another ECG and Stress Test at Edgecliff got the all clear. I saw an Indian Doctor at Hurstville who recommended acupuncture and exercises and a practitioner for Lymphatic Drainage Massages. I was going off balance and had a CT neck scan and back x-ray. As usual nothing showed up.

I journeyed to Eastwood to a Chiropractor/Osteopath and another Kinesiologist, the search just went on and on, I felt there must have been an answer somewhere. In October I went to Thailand again and had my usual Thai Massage every day, it worked wonders for the pain in my body but my nights were still disturbed with vibrations, wakefulness and loose bowel movements. Luckily I could sleep during the day. One of my favourite past times is sleeping on a beach. It does wonders for me. Over the years I also listened to relaxation and meditation tapes, sometimes during the night they would put me to sleep but others I remained wide awake. If I used all the techniques I had been taught, I would be doing nothing else all day and night.

Many books have helped me over the years but To See Differently by Susan Trout was a work book, which I followed carefully. It is a wonderful self help book.

Some of my writings, I feel, are worth recording here.

INNER PEACE.

Inner peace means being at peace with myself. To love and accept myself as I am. To have a calm mind, to think clearly, what is best for my highest good and the highest good of all? Inner peace is a state of mind, where healing takes place. Where unconditional love is experienced and put into practice. It feels as if I am in tune with my own energy and higher self. I have no need to judge myself or others or situations. I feel at peace with the universe. I have experienced it in moments of meditation, sometimes on a beach or a tranquil scene in nature. I would like to experience it now, when I am in pain and fearful of what this could lead to, when I feel insecure about the future. Lack of trust and connection to my higher self keeps me from doing that. To come back to my inner self by calming my breathing, my mind and reconnecting to my inner being.

LOVING KINDNESS.

Loving kindness means being thoughtful of my own and others needs and sensitivities. Sharing your love in kind ways. Sending loving thoughts to those you love, as well as those whose opinions and ideas clash with yours or those who you believe have hurt you in some way. Radiating loving kindness to all beings, means wishing them no harm, wishing them well, asking that they be happy and peaceful . . . free from enmity, anger and suffering. Experiencing loving kindness gives me a rosy glow in my heart, the warmth of knowing I am loving to myself and others. I have experienced it in small ways a big ways when I have empowered someone. When someone has responded and mirrored back to me my loving kindness. I would like to express it more to my closest relations but find it easier with friends or even total strangers. What keeps me from doing it, is fear of rejection, not being accepted, taken the wrong way or feeling unloved. I can remind myself to practise this quality on myself by being mindful and thoughtful to me or others when I feel tension in the air, or when a kind word is needed. I give out to my family by communicating more frequently and at a deeper level, speaking my truth, my feelings with mindfulness to create peace and harmony.

HAPPINESS.

Happiness means feeling at peace with myself and the world. Being with those I love. Doing things for those I love or total strangers in need. Happiness is joy, laughter, being myself, not wearing a mask, letting it all hangout, feeling freedom, being generous, not having expectations, accepting what is, writing letters, keeping in touch with friends by email, receiving letters from overseas and local friends, being able to stand up for myself with kindness, being in touch with my intuitive side, feeling good about myself, listening and really hearing, remembering what people have said and enquiring about it later. Feeling happy is like being held up by a big wave in the ocean, supported, free, light, surrounded by beauty and nature, strength and change. I have felt happiness when I have been understood and listened to by a friend, when I have laughed with friends and family till my nose has run, my face has turned purple and my eyes have watered. When I think of my son in Canada and the beautiful granddaughter he has given me . . . what a gift. I swell with pride when I think of how well my two kids have done in life. Their achievements and happiness are my happiness. The euphoria of their birth . . . blissful . . . breath taking happy experiences. I would like to express more happiness in the world for others to share. I sometimes feel daunted and overwhelmed at times by the atrocities that are taking place in the world. The best thing I can do is remind myself to be happy by changing my negative thoughts to positive thoughts. I can think of the joy my children bring me.

HEALING.

Healing means love of mind, body and spirit, balancing and healing of emotions, mental thoughts, all senses. To be at peace with oneself and the environment, the world, the universe. To heal is to remedy, to remedy is to bring back balance, to find that place within you, to be centred, have homeostasis in the physical body. It feels like a state of bliss, non attachment to material things or even physical pain. Detachment from others opinions and thoughts, non judgement of yourself and others. Learning to give without expectations of what you will receive in return. Feeling good about yourself, accepting that this is the way it is right now. Healing feels like when you are in touch with universal wisdom and knowing. Going with the flow, not swimming against the tide. I have experienced healing when I have forgiven myself and others, when I have let go of some perceived wrong towards me. In Epidavros in an amphitheatre in Greece, when I felt I had come home. In Bodh Gaya in India where the Buddha was enlightened, sitting under the bodhi tree meditating. In Koh Samet in Thailand sitting on my porch watching the sunrise, looking at the rippling waters, reflecting the sun in spasms. I would like to experience healing right now and in every present moment. In the night when I feel fearful and shaky, in a panic attack. Lack of connection with my divine inner self prevents me from experiencing this. I will meditate to centre myself and get in touch with my inner being.

COMPASSION.

Compassion means showing you care and feel passionate about someone or something. Going the extra mile in caring, really putting yourself in others shoes, showing empathy, being in touch with where they are coming from, being tender with oneself and others, being thoughtful, seeing the need and acting on it. It feels warm and fuzzy to experience compassion. It comes from the heart . . . not with expectations of the outcome, not with expectations of what's in it for me. A genuine feeling of deep unconditional love. I have experienced it in small and overwhelmingly large ways, when someone has been particularly compassionate towards me, when I have done some small nice deeds for someone and they haven't known who did it. When a friend invites me to dinner after I have been massaging all day, when my daughter comes to my work place to help me lock up and walks home with me. I would like to feel compassion when I have lost the ability to give myself unconditional love. Lack of wise thoughts prevents me from doing that. I lose the connection to my inner being. I could remind myself to practise this inner quality by taking time to stop and go within. Knowing that what you give out, you get back tenfold.

EQUANIMITY

Equanimity to me means getting the balance, being equal, experiencing the yin and yang, the good and the bad, the positive and the negative, the pain and the healing. To experience equanimity is to be in balance in your life, your mind, your thoughts and your feelings, to be at peace with the universe, to be in peace when all about you is chaos. I have experienced equanimity in my life when I have not taken on other people's projections or problems, when I have been honest and true to myself. When I have stood up for what I believe, when my energies have been in balance, not too high, not too low, when I have had a deep meditation and feel calm and peaceful. When I am with people who I love and who love me. I would like to express myself when situations get out of balance, when my mind is not at peace, to be able to restore harmony in chaos. I am out of balance when I am not accepting others as they are, when I am judging myself and not accepting that this is the way it is right now. What keeps me from doing that? Lack of connection with my inner self and divine being. I need to remind myself to practise this quality of equanimity I can stop, ask myself what I can do to bring back the balance. I need to forgive myself and others and all past experiences. Let go of guilt and shame. Be aware, awake and conscious. Accept that this is the way it is and everything changes, nothing is permanent.

2000

At the beginning 0f 2000 I did a road trip to Queensland in a camper van with my son, daughter-in-law, her parents and my one year old granddaughter. It was challenging but fun. I had learned to accept that the vibrations, palpitations and rapid heartbeat were part of life. I was determined that the panic attacks would not stop me from what I wanted to do and that was to live life to the fullest. The pain in my neck, ribcage and thoracic area, were eased a bit by a Chiropractor at Airlie Beach in Queensland.

When I got home, I started a part time job massaging and caring for a lady who had a stroke some years before and was in a wheel chair. I massaged part time in a clinic and my other part time clients as well as friends and relations from home. I was determined to carry on a productive and interesting life, an important part of which was being of service to others, despite a few new ailments creeping into my body. I experienced pain in my sacrum, palms of my hands and soles of my feet and the skin went red and then started peeling off, sharp abdominal spasms, sometimes getting up six or seven times in the night to urinate. My hair started falling out. There were some occasional days when I felt great, I really relished these days and was so grateful for them. I continued to take vitamins, minerals, homeopathics, Swedish bitters, Siberian Ginseng, Poke root, cordyceps and flaxseed oil. I saw numerous muscular/skeletal doctors, GP's, Chiropractic/Kinesiologists, spiritual healers, pranic and polarity healers.

There was an advertisement in an Eastern Suburbs Magazine that a trial was being held for people who are experiencing panic attacks. It was organised by Macquarie University, I contacted them and started on the program with a work book, recording my symptoms and what brought them on etc. For some months I liaised with the Clinical Psychologist who was in charge of collecting all the data and I was given a copy of the work book *Panic Surfing: A self treatment workbook for panic disorder,* through Cognitive Behaviour Therapy to help you deal with panic. We were meant to try to trigger an attack. This was impossible for me as I was always woken in the night by the attack. I did not go to bed thinking 'I hope I don't have an attack tonight'. I had no real phobias or fears, I was determined that the panic attacks were not going to rule my life in any way. We were told to call the symptoms 'sensations' rather than symptoms, not to let an attack consume you. Ride it like a wave, out of 500 attacks, everyone has come out of it intact. I've been through worse times and not lost control. Bipolar and schizophrenia do not start with panic attacks. That was good to hear, as there was bipolar in my family and I certainly did not want to go down that track. I also learned that 25% of nocturnal panic attacks come out of REM sleep and

75% from second stage sleep. I wrote down how I felt about challenging thoughts, to get them out of my head and more able to deal with them, really explore them. I was to tell the negative thoughts to GET OUT, time and again. Some of the thoughts and feelings that I had was that I was helpless, vulnerable, out of control, scared and that worse was to come. I was fed up and frustrated because I seldom felt 'normal'. I was fed up with unidentified pain, fed up with the hideous expense of it all and still not finding answers.

After working my way through the workbook, I was asked to attend five two hour group sessions with other people experiencing panic attacks. This was a challenge, because I could not relate to their sensations. For a start, I was the oldest in the group by about thirty years and my attacks had not commenced after smoking marihuana or taking 'social' drugs. I did not have a fear of going in lifts, on escalators, heights, crowds or being alone while in the shower and having to have a family member in the bathroom. I was not overly fearful of public speaking or acting in a stage performance. While I did learn a lot about coping with the panic attacks and they did diminish to a degree, they certainly had not left me completely.

2001

The year started off with a camping trip to the Country Music Festival at Tamworth, in north western New England area on NSW. It was extremely hot and exhausting, rushing from singing performances to bush poets and doing Line Dancing. In fact, my friends and I managed to get into the Guinness Book of Records by being three of the participants in the World Record number of 6600 people Line Dancing in the main street of Tamworth. The neck and lumbar spine pains kept me awake at night, rapid heartbeats and fluttering of my upper lip was unnerving. I never knew what sensations were going to crop up next.

My daughter moved to Goorambat in Victoria in February, I went to help her unpack and get settled into a lovely old home she was renting out of town. Each day we would take a break and swim in the river at Benalla, nearby, and I would do my Qi Gong. One night I was woken by feeling shaky, my legs wobbly, palpitations of the heart and blurred vision. I was totally disorientated and unable to get back to sleep. I managed an afternoon nap, which was always a pick-me-up.

At home I started soaking my feet in salt baths before I went to bed, this was helpful on some nights. I also took magnesium powder for the leg cramps which plagued me during sleep. The heat in my face continued from time to time, as did the thoracic spasms after getting breathless then sitting down. None of the doctors, practitioners that I saw had an answer for these. I averaged six panic attacks a month for the year, ranging from mild to moderately severe. Averaged sixteen hours of massaging clients a month, sixteen times a month doing Qi Gong, played tennis three to four times a month and sixteen times a month for a swim, either in rivers, lakes, the beach or a pool.

In May I got a Round the World ticket and travelled alone to Thailand, Hungary, Austria, Greece, Germany, Sudbury and Vancouver in Canada for two months. In Germany I found a tick had burrowed into my stomach, luckily I was staying with a friend, who knew all about these little blighters. She had a special implement to remove the tick and a solution to pour in the hole. We had been walking the dog in the forest and had seen deer and gone skinny dipping in a lake, which was great fun. The danger being that deer in this part of the world carry Limes disease and it can be transmitted to humans through ticks. Good fortune was with me and there were no ill effects. In Hungary I enjoyed many occasions of dunking my body in the thermal baths and having massages. These certainly helped the pain in my left ribcage which was going into my breast. A chiropractor, in Sydney, explained that it was probably a scar tissue injury from an old fall. Could it have been the horse fall in 1985?

In Canada, I had times of feeling lousy and lacked energy after disrupted nights of body pulsations and disorientation.

A local Bondi GP/Iridologist took some blood tests and found I had Candida and low Vitamin B12. I had a few sessions of Kinegetics and Korean Ki Energy massage, which was interesting and I continued to take Rock Rose and Aspen homeopathics, slippery elm, Swedish Bitters, chromium, Tresos B, St Marys Thistle, lipoec, kelp, flaxseed oil, Vitamin E and CoQ 10. The early morning bowel movements continued, any time between 2–4am. It was often difficult to get back to sleep. A strange fluttering started in my muscles. I never knew which part of my body it was going to appear in next. Rescue Remedy was never far from my bed and hand bag.

A muscular/skeletal GP gave me acupuncture which relieved a lot of my aches and pains. My casual part time caring jobs, massage, Qi Gong, tennis, body surfing, swimming, all kept me busy and it was difficult at times to keep my energy levels up. At times I felt 'washed out'.

October found me in Cambodia with a friend. While it was extremely hot and humid and the days exhausting, I really enjoyed Ankor Wat with all its amazing aged temples and interesting history. I had some bad nights of shaking, chest pain and left rib pain. I had some wonderful massages from blind people. Mainly they had lost their sight when land mines had exploded, as they unknowingly stepped on them in the fields. I found the Cambodians beautiful, caring people. I finished off this trip with two weeks on my favourite Thai island, where I am always more at peace and comfortable, with only minor sensations of panic disorders. One late afternoon as I had my shower before dinner, I began to cry, it was totally unprovoked and out of the blue, it went on and on, I was just in floods of tears. I did not try to stop it, I had never experienced anything like it before but I felt it was best to just go with it. Afterwards, although I felt wrung out, I also felt cleansed somehow.

After Christmas I participated in a Meditation Retreat at the Sunnataram Forest Monastery at Bundanoon for a week. Meditation for me was survival . . . and still is. I believe it was the main thing in my life that helped me to cope.

2002

Early in the year I answered a Patient Questionnaire for Dental Toxicity Assessment. To quote the first paragraph: *This questionnaire is part of a 1996 US FDA approved study called an institutional Review Board to assess how body burden of mercury is determined, toxicity levels etc. It will serve as a warning/alert to clinicians **when patients have scores of 'yes 'in five or more questions**. It is recommended that such patients be referred to dentists with special knowledge of safe mercury amalgam removal and replacement.*

Out of the 30 questions, I ticked 20 'Yes' and 10 'No'.

Some of the questions that scored a yes were: Have you had symptoms such as confusion, forgetfulness, depression, ringing in your ears, shakiness in hands or arms, twitching muscles. Do you have 'brown spots' or 'age spots' under your eyes or elsewhere, food allergies or intolerances, more than ten amalgam fillings, have you worked as a dental assistant (20 years), Candida, white tongue, low body temperature, mucous in your stools, heart irregularities, rapid pulse, unexplained joint pain, chest pains, frequent insomnia, fatigue.

Removing dental amalgams is a very specialised field, if not done correctly it can be really dangerous to your health. After much research and consultation with a few specialist dentists, I chose one in Gordon, Sydney. It was three years after I first saw the above questionnaire that I decided to meditate through the amalgam removal and not have my mouth numbed by local anaesthetic. The dentist was comfortable with this, as he was a meditator himself. The four two hour sessions where accompanied by intravenous vitamin C and a saline drip, administered by a doctor, an oxygen mask for me and the dentist also. I had a compatibility test before the amalgams were replaced, just to make sure they were not replaced with another substance that was not agreeable to my system. A week after the last appointment I went to India. I was really happy to be rid of all that mercury. I had also been breathing in mercury vapour for twenty years, having been a full time chair side assistant for nine years and a part time dental health educator for eleven.

In India I went, for the second time, to see Satya Sai Baba, a much admired guru and healer with followers from all over the world. It is always quite an amazing experience but I was no further along the path for a cure for my panic disorder. I also had a very different massage, where the masseuse used about a litre of oil to splash over my body with a gentle rub. I felt like a seal on a glazed surface and was fearsome when turning over that I did not land with a moist wallop on the floor.

Before having a shower, she scattered some white powder over my body, you can imagine the combination of that with the oil. I stood under the shower for about fifteen minutes trying to get some semblance of finding my normal skin.

I ventured south to Goa by numerous forms of transport including trains, buses, rickshaws, backs of trucks and motor bikes. Having torn a ligament in my left knee earlier in the year, I suffered some very painful days and nights, even though applying my favourite Chinese Herbal Lotion Zhen Gu Shui and sometimes using it as a poultice. On a forty one hour train trip from Goa to New Delhi, my left leg got really swollen. What with little personal space and some minor panic sensations, I didn't get much sleep, none the less, it is always interesting travelling with the masses in India. This long trip cost me AUD$14.45 and I got a Seniors Discount. Can't complain about that.

Another train and bus journey found me in Dharamsala in the north of India. The World Health Organisation was holding an open day with free healings and exciting games like hoopla and shooting at balloons. In the latter, I excelled and was the only female to have a go, but the former I was not quite so accurate. I went to the Tibetan Medicine Doctor to find my blood pressure was 120/80, she also did a pulse diagnosis and said my general health was fine. She sent me away with some Tibetan Herbs for my constitution. The whole consultation cost me AUD$1.50. I was responsible for removing a cow from the field, which had placed itself in the middle of everything. In India, the cattle know they are sacred and I hope I did not offend any bovine gods by pulling its head around, slapping it on the rump and directing it to the exit. The crowd cheered, so I can't have been all bad.

I also had the supreme honour and pleasure of shaking the hand and getting a blessing from HH the Dalai Lama. That really was the highlight of this trip. A bus and train ride to Varanasi took me to a small two star hotel, right on the Ganges and right beside the second largest burning ghat. Not for the faint hearted, nor was the massage I had at the hotel, it was more of a rolling pin pummelling, which was bad enough, but when he took to the soles of my feet with a wire brush, I indicated I had had enough. I heard about a sadhu, holy man, on the banks of the river who does numerology and astrology. His cave like room was at the very top on the many steps leading up from the river. My knee was by no means healed and I was in agony by the time I made it to the oversized closet that he worked from. He told me some interesting and true facts about my life and told me to come back tomorrow to pick up some Ayurvedic oil for my knee. It was a challenge getting up the steps the next day and the oil smelt foul and rancid but I figured that it was worth a try. I used it for some weeks before the smell finally got to me and I disposed of it in a bin.

The train ride to Gaya was in a second class sleeper and I was astonished to see clean sheets, a pillow and blanket, even a reading light in my four berth carriage. The only other occupant was an Indian Sikh man with very good English. We talked most of the way until our arrival at midnight in Gaya where I checked into the Classic Hotel for AUD$6 a night. The room at the Buddhagaya Thai Monastery was even cheaper at AUD$4.50 a night. The temperature was 42 degrees so I kept the fan going all night but my sleep was light and disturbed. During the day I would sit in the town square and massage necks, shoulders, arms, knees for the locals, while sitting under a shady tree. The queues got long and the days got hotter. At night I felt strange and kept going off balance. There was a mouse plague, they were in and out of everything, including buckets of water that I was to use as my shower. The kitchen was overrun with them, gorging on wheat and rice through holes in the sacks, dashing in and out of cooking utensils and crockery. It is a miracle that I did not get sick. A dog took to me with great friendship and slept under my bed. I had a continuing dream that I was living in an old dilapidated farmhouse, the floors were packed mud, the furniture was packing cases and animals ran in and out. Over the years I have had this dream with slight variations many times. I finished this trip off with a few days in Calcutta to catch up with my Anglo Indian friends then went to Koh Samet in Thailand, my favourite island. Here I have a daily massage, do my meditation and Qi Gong every morning and swim in the crystal clear waters off white sand beaches, eat Thai food to my heart's content . . . it is bliss. I wrote in my diary that my Thai massage, given by my Thai friend of twenty years 'is the closest thing to heaven without going through the pearly gates'.

Frequent urination disturbed my nights, one night I counted seven trips to the bathroom and the pain in my left knee was always worse in bed at night. Why is that so? An afternoon nap was quite often possible and very much needed. My time at Koh Samet was all too short but I count my blessings and savour every moment of my 'home away from home'. When I got home in mid May I had these 'bubbling' feelings in my chest, which was weird but by now I am learning that this is the way it is right now and accept that nothing lasts forever. I had trips to Wollongong and Narooma before going to Queensland for five days with my daughter. I was taking kelp, selenium, magnesium oratate, de-mer-tox, Vitamin C and E, chlorella, bio zinc, Vitamin B complex, St Marys Thistle, chlorella, glucosamine, nilstat, chondromine, gingko biloba, gentian, colloidal silver and toxicol. There is hardly a mineral or vitamin or supplement that I have not been prescribed at some stage of my existence.

A Chinese Doctor in the city was recommended to me in June and he prescribed Chinese Herbs, so I added those to the mix. I also had acupuncture, moxabustion, cupping and foot massage over some months of treatment. My upper thoracic pain, neck, shoulder and occipital pain continued to haunt me and the neck and shoulder sweats in the night were annoying and disturbing. On a good note, my knee was gradually getting better. I continued to massage part time, do Qi Gong, swim and sometimes play tennis and of course meditate.

In July I went to another of my favourite places, Belongil Beach, just north of Byron Bay after staying for a few days with a friend in South Golden Beach, another lovely northern beach. My friend was keen for me to go bike riding with him, I had been told that it is good therapy for knee problems. While I managed to do it, it did stir my knee up a bit. While there I had some iridology and experienced dowsing, listened to Caroline Myss tapes every day and went in the surf. I also saw numerous dolphins and whales, they too help to heal the soul. In Byron Bay I bought myself a stuffed, very life like, blue cattle dog, I named him Barney. He caused quite a sensation on the train on the way home and more so when I sat him on a chair at afternoon tea at the retirement village in Bondi Beach where I live. Some of the old dears nearly freaked out, thinking he was real. He still lives in my bedroom and is a great listener and constant companion.

It is no wonder that the years go by so quickly for me, I do tend to pack a lot into my interesting and enjoyable life. In August I set off for Canada, firstly staying with a really good friend on Vancouver Island. She is Austrian and married to an Australia but they have been living in Canada for many years. They now live on a small lake just out of Victoria, so we swam often and I ventured out on the paddle boat, as a fun adventure, as I am a rank beginner at it. Our days are never dull, going for long bike rides down fire trails and through forests. We talk late into each night, as there is a lot of catching up to do. My visits to the bathroom are less frequent, thank goodness. After a week when my friend put me on the ferry from Naniamo back to Vancouver, I slept all the way. When I left for Toronto on the plane, I was asleep before takeoff. I arrived in Sudbury to stay with my son, daughter in law and two grandchildren now, fully rested and ready to enjoy life on Birch Lake. I sleep in a log cabin only metres from the lake, so am up early most mornings to see the sunrise and make some noise, so that the two snakes living underneath me know not to appear. I experience the heat in my face from time to time and my nights are not so disturbed but I do have some pretty weird dreams. Here I paddle a canoe and one day my son and I went out in it and as usual got quite hysterical. He has made me laugh ever since he was a baby. Of course laughter is very good for pain release. I also spent a lot of time in the hot tub on the veranda and found it very good for any aches and pains in joints and muscles.

I did have a bad panic attack one night but had the Rescue Remedy with me and eventually went back to sleep. Always feel very washed out the next day and had mild vibrations throughout my body the following night. Over the years I have learned not to be so terrified by the unusual sensations and know that eventually they will pass. I am always sad to leave my family behind in Canada but am also very grateful for the joy they bring me and the fun we have when I am with them. I am truly blessed.

The panic attacks continued throughout the year, with four or five a month always accompanied by heat in my face, my left arm feeling heavy, rapid heartbeats, vibrations through my body, sometimes pain in my thoracic area and the left side of my face going numb, my left eye being hard to open in the morning. Mostly a bowel movement in the middle of the night.

My four day trip to Melbourne went well in October, my main purpose of the visit was to see my daughter play volleyball in the Masters Game. My left knee persisted in causing me pain, in fact enough for me to give up tennis for a while. I still managed to massage and do Qi Gong and ride my bike on a regular basis.

In November I went to a doctor in Edgecliff for several sessions of acupuncture, unfortunately with not much benefit. I also saw another Listen System practitioner with much the same result. I went to the city to have a thermogram of my upper body, which is less invasive than a mammogram, all was well.

The Bali bombing took place in October, I felt I needed to give some support to the beautiful Balinese people. So many of them lost their lives and of course many Australians also, it was a terrible tragedy. The Australian Government was suggesting travellers should not go to Bali and as a consequence many planes were cancelled. I managed to leave on Friday 13th December, I suppose no one wants to travel on Friday 13th but it was my only option. The only date I was able to get a return flight was four weeks later. On arriving in Denpasar I registered with the Red Cross as a volunteer and donated blood, which was in short supply. I also visited survivors and their families in hospital, as I had taken a bag full of toys to hand out. A female doctor was very good to me and ferried me round on the back of her motorbike to see her sister who is a spiritual healer. This lady told me not to drink alcohol, to eat only fruit and vegetables, not to go to a doctor because I can heal myself. I was also to soak my feet and lower legs in salt water before going to bed at night. I am to cut down on massaging and make sure to wash my hands and arms up to the elbows after I have massaged anyone. My aura is good and I am to continue meditating every day and do yoga three times a week. She would not accept any money, which was really nice of her. Everywhere I went I found such kindness and compassion. I managed to massage some of the young men working and job sharing at my guesthouse, so many are out of work and depression has really set in. I paid a short visit to Ubud and put my name down to volunteer but was not contacted. All I can do is spend as much money as I can buying presents for family and friends, to try to boost the economy in a small way. Booked a boat trip on a small 20 passenger boat leaving from Lombok for five days, we visit Perama Island, which only has a hut on it, we snorkel and I am bitten by a red jelly fish, luckily not a deadly variety. At Satonda Island we are greeted by an 80 year old ranger, who lives on his own on the island, we swim in a magnificent crater lake and watch the monkeys frolic in the nearby trees. On to Sambawa Island we walk to a village about five kilometres away, through very fine dust, in Australia we call it bulldust, the locals are all smiling happily and we sing nursery rhymes for the children. The dark clouds arrive very quickly and we have to take a short cut back to the beach to get the boat. We half swim half cling to the cliffs over sharp volcanic rocks, and at one stage we have to jump a ravine, only sheer terror and strong mindfulness gets me across, my sandals fell to bits just as we came to a beach with broken coral, loose rocks, shells and driftwood. In the water some delightful dolphins put on a magical display for us. It makes the hardships all worthwhile. We spend Christmas Day walking on Komodo Island and get up close and personal with the Komodo Dragons, only the ones that have just been fed. On our walk we see four of these dragons devouring a pig carcass, bones and all. It is hot and humid and I am the oldest by about twenty years but I manage to keep up.

I do some massages on the boat for some tired and aching bodies before we arrive at Flores, where I can purchase some new thongs. On board that night we eat the last of the live chickens that have been on the boat, so we know they are fresh! We celebrate Christmas with balloons, horns and whistles and party hats, the crew joins us in singing and dancing. Certainly a Christmas with a difference and one to remember. On our way to Rinca island, while I am on the loo, a large rat ran down a pipe beside me. We see more Komodo Dragons here, the landscape is hilly with palm trees and cactus and large shade trees, which the dragons sensibly rest under. We walk for three hours in the heat of the day in clinging mud, my new thongs stand up to the rough treatment. A physiotherapist fellow adventurer gives me a massage, which is great before we get to Gili Laba (Spider Island) where we snorkel and swim and I do my Qi Gong on the beach. Moyo Island is our next stop, where we walk through shaded trees, crossing streams, waterfalls and seeing water buffaloes wallowing in mud. We arrive back in Lombok tired but happy. I spend another week on Gili Air and celebrate the New Year with locals and am so pleased not to have had a panic attack on this journey.

2003

For some reason I am hesitant to start writing about this year, maybe because it is the year that I found the healer who helped me to end my panic attacks forever. After eight long years my search for a solution comes to an end.

My journey to Bali ended in January, I arrived home and a few days later I was running a high temperature, I even resorted to taking some Panadol. You may have gathered by now that I am reluctant to take drugs of any kind. I drank six glasses of filtered water every morning to keep hydrated. My energy levels were very low and I was going off balance, everything I ate tasted awful, I was succumbing to afternoon sleeps, as my night sleep pattern was totally disturbed. I soaked my feet in salt water before bedtime to little advantage. A Bondi Junction Chiropractor used some cranio/sacral treatment on me and a friend from Bundanoon took me through some Life Management sessions, I was always eager to learn and anxious to help heal myself. The saying 'physician heal thyself' was upper most in my mind. I believed I could do it.

By February the skin on the palms of my hands and soles of my feet went red and finally white and then started peeling off, still I battled on massaging and having some good Chinese Massage myself, as my lumbar area and sciatic nerve were causing me pain. My left thigh was going numb when standing for any time and my legs felt weak, at times I had to find somewhere to sit down. I had mild pain in my lower abdomen. I was experiencing panic attacks nearly once a week.

In March I went to Narooma, on the south coast, to stay with friends for five days, but continued to have good and bad nights, also sharp pain in my left ribs and breast area. Sometimes I took half a Valium to get some undisturbed sleep, because I felt so wrung out during the day. I started taking silica, slippery elm, ecanachea, poke root, ginger, garlic, honey, lemon and cayenne pepper, turmeric and coriander. A South Korean gave me a Ki Massage, which was interesting and we chatted about the different techniques of massage around the world, I also went to a Natural Therapies Day in Chatswood and had iridology. As my knee was improving, I took up tennis again, I love the game and find the social side fun too. I walked and swam as often as possible and went in the surf to catch a few waves, I find the salt water is like a detox, soothing the mind, body and spirit. I continued to have Neurolink with the Chiropractor, ride an exercise bike, do Qi Gong, stretch, meditate and have computer lessons. I had been emailing for some years but wanted to expand my internet knowledge. A friend and I even took motorised bicycles by train and bus to the Bundanoon is Brigadoon Festival and rode to Moss Vale and down Bondi Road through the traffic, with no lights at 10pm. A Relationship Workshop was very helpful and in May I did a thirteen week course of The Artist's Way, facilitated by a really good friend of mine. It is based on the book by Julia Cameron and I can really recommend it for anyone wanting to find their creative side and really deal with life's issues, past and present. One of the criteria is to write Three Pages each morning, as soon as you wake up, they can be about anything and everything, positive, negative, whatever comes into your head, or dialogue a conversation that you need to have or have had. In fact just write.

The World Laughter Day was run in May at Glebe, little did I know that later this year I would find myself at a Laughter Training Workshop and be running the Bondi Beach Laughter Club for the next seven years. Mind you I have been a giggler and laugher all my life, so it was not so hard for me to step into such a whacky field.

The vibrations in my upper body continued to shake me up, also palpitations and sometimes my hands going numb were pretty scary, as were some severe stabbing pains in my sternum and thoracic area. In the month of May I had eight panic attacks but still managed to do the Artist's Way classes, walk with friends from Bondi Beach to Circular Quay, walk home from Watsons Bay and attend the Sydney Writers Festival, where I had been a volunteer for some years. I have been told by doctors and practitioners over the years that I have a good constitution and stamina, one even told me I 'come from good solid stock'. No doubt that does help. Some of the other supplements I took over the year were Vitamin E and C, Magnesium Ortotate, Zinc,

Silicon, colloidal silver, flaxseed, spiralina, chlorella, toxicol, tresos B, olive leaf extract and gentian.

June was a really challenging month where I experienced thirteen panic attacks. Sometimes I found myself writing my Three Morning Pages at 3am, unable to sleep with disturbing dreams and thoughts, pain in my body, twitching in my muscles, palpitations in my heart, vibrations throughout my body, sweating in my neck and shoulders and heat in my face. One would have thought that my blood pressure was sky high but when I took it one day, it was 130/82, not too bad. Trying to convince myself that these sensations were not going to create a heart attack or stroke was sometimes very demanding, on the other hand, going through medical tests and everything coming up normal, was apt to leave the medical fraternity believing I was ready for the nut house! I, on occasions, was asking myself, 'am I imaging all this' but it was way too real to think that. I was determined to keep up my daily routines of exercising, massaging, meditating and doing Qi Gong, sometimes pushing myself to the limits.

In July I turned sixty five and the panic attacks only occurred five times. I visited the Byron Bay Writers Festival with friends and stayed in one of my favourite places, Belongil Beach, a peaceful, beautiful area with healing energy. It was while staying here that I heard of an Esoteric Healer who had helped a friend of my mine release her panic attacks. I also had trips to Bowral and the Monastery at Bundanoon, closer to home I attended Spirituality in the Pub, always an interesting experience. I enjoyed a guided tour of the Great Synagogue and a healing session at St Andrews Cathedral in Sydney. I really searched and researched the answers to my problem, never giving up and always knowing in the back of my mind that I would one day find a solution to these very debilitating attacks and sensations.

As August came around, I completed The Artist's Way course and visited my daughter in Melbourne, staying with friends in Wangaratta and Beechworth on the way, the panic attacks continued and I made a decision not to write any more sensations down, I wondered if I was giving power to them by always focusing on them.

In early September I saw a Psychologist and had some hypnotherapy, I continued to be a blood donor but that stopped when I got Shingles in my left eye, in my nose and my ear and up into my forehead and hair, the latter diminishing in handfuls and leaving a funny gap in my head and even funnier look in my eyes. After seeing an eye specialist who predicted I would have partial vision for about six months, I proved him wrong by having my old vision back in a couple of weeks. This eye specialist related an interesting story to me of how he nearly lost his vision when a runaway horse took him under a thorny tree, as a kid, in Moss Vale. I immediately came clean and told him it probably happened at my family home and riding school. He was amazed at the coincidence and I was able to fill him in on some of the details of hawthorn trees, he said he always wondered what type of tree it was. I succumbed to Panedeine for the pain, antibiotics for any infection and specialised drugs for Shingles.

On 20th September I made an appointment, in Sydney, with the Esoteric Healer I had heard about in Byron Bay in July. I must say, I had seen so many practitioners that I did not have too much faith in this treatment being any different but I always left myself open to the prospect that one day I would find the perfect solution. All it took was one hour, ONE HOUR and I was released from panic attacks, that I had been living and struggling with for eight long arduous years, for ever more. Those years that caused me so much anguish, doubt, horrific fear, sleepless nights, exhausting days, absolute terror, panic, fear of the unknown, zapping my strength my energy and my life, are now a thing of the past.

There is not a day that goes by that I am not grateful to that Esoteric Healer, who turned my life around. When he first looked at me he said 'you have been going through hell', I nearly wept, here was someone who understood and didn't think I was crazy or ready for the nut house. When I walked out the door and said my profound thanks, his words were 'you won't need to see me again'. To be honest, there was a slight feeling of scepticism, because I had seen so many practitioners, spent so much money, time and effort but somewhere deep down inside of my being, I knew there was truth in what he told me.

How free my life has been since then, how glorious the days and especially the nights, how great it feels to have energy to support others on their journey and live my life to the full. No doubt everyone has many aspects of their lives with peaks and troughs, mine has been a journey of extremes in a way, of complete changes in direction, challenges and adventures of the mind, body and spirit.

About the Author

Noni Gove grew up in her family home in the Southern Highlands of NSW Australia. She has a Diploma of Dental Assisting and numerous Diplomas in many forms of Remedial Therapeutic Massage. She is interested in alternate therapies, the mind and how it operates.